JANE SMISOR BASTIEN ♦ LISA BAST[...]N

A DEBUT FOR YOU

Book 3

TO THE PIANISTS

If you are preparing for your first performance in a special situation, then you will be making your debut. *Debut* is a French word, pronounced *day BYOO.*

Maybe you've already had your debut playing for other students of your piano teacher, but we hope you will have many more debuts in your life–perhaps playing for your class in school, or for your grandparents, or for parties.

We hope that you will love playing these pieces whether it's for a debut or not!

CONTENTS

ISBN 0-8497-9530-3

©1993 Neil A. Kjos Music Company, 4380 Jutland Drive, San Diego, California 92117.
International copyright secured. All rights reserved. Printed in U.S.A.

Early to Rise

Lori Bastien

When you wake up ver-y ear-ly you will find that the morn-ing's real-ly great!

Greet each new day on a good note bright and ear-ly— nev-er, nev-er late!

Double Ferris Wheel

Jane Smisor Bastien

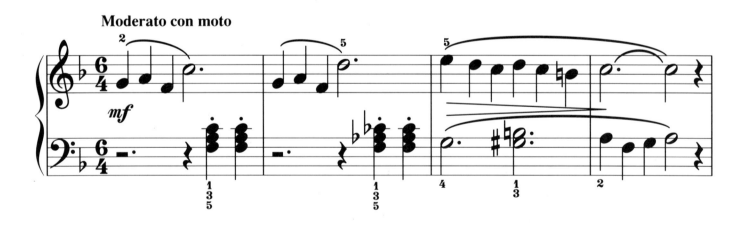

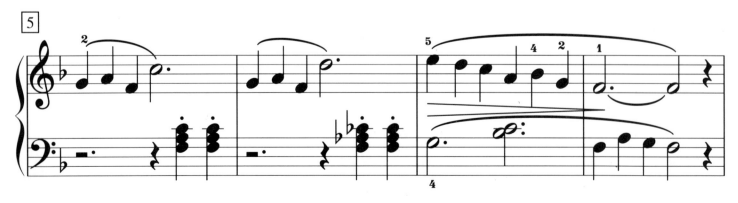

Faded Blue Jeans

Lori Bastien

South of Our Border

Lori Bastien

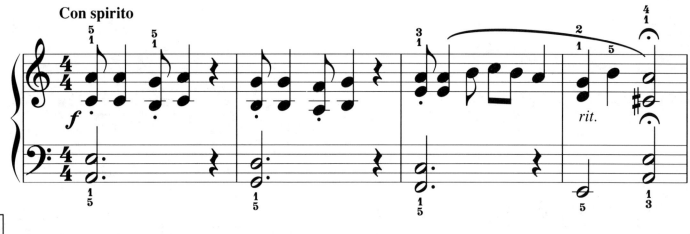

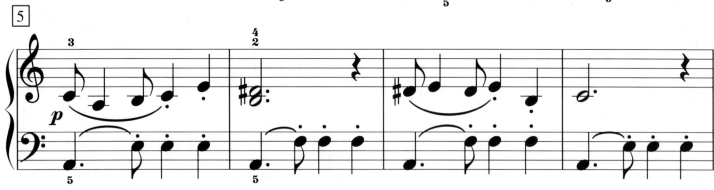

Hearts from Heaven

Lisa Bastien

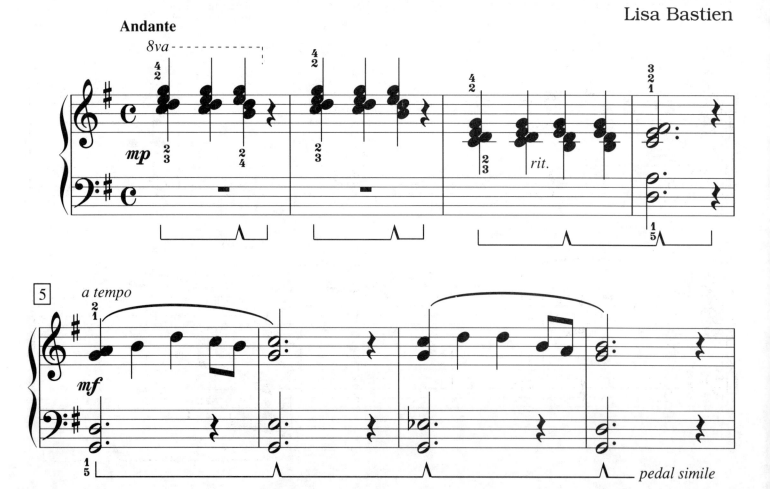

Overnight Camp

Lori Bastien

Moderato

f This is the first time I've been a-way from home, I'm hav-ing so much fun!

5 Thought I'd be lone-ly, not know a sin-gle soul, but I soon met ev-'ry one!

9 *mf* We have break-fast at eight, then take hikes.

Hangin' Out at the Mall

Jane Smisor Bastien

Con moto

mf Let's get to-geth-er this week-end.___ We can hang out at the mall.___

It's our last chance be-fore school starts___ to buy new clothes for the fall.___

f Can't be-lieve how fast the time flies, This sum-mer's real-ly been great.___

Dancing in My Dreams

Lisa Bastien

The Great Chase

Jane Smisor Bastien

Hang Ten Rock

Lisa Bastien

The Dynamic Detectives

Lisa Bastien

ABOUT THE COMPOSERS

Jane Smisor Bastien

Jane Smisor Bastien and her husband, James, have written many piano books over the years for elementary students. Jane still maintains a full teaching schedule in her home in La Jolla, California.

The Bastiens' writing career began years ago when Jane needed music for her pre-school beginners. Because there wasn't an appropriate method she wrote her own to use with the small class of four- and five-year-old beginners she was teaching. Lisa, their first child, was in the class. By the time their second child Lori was four, Jane's method–*The Very Young Pianist Library* was published.

As Lisa and Lori grew up they witnessed the stream of students who learned in the Bastien home studio. They became teaching assistants at an early age and during their high school (and college) years they had their own students. They spent their high school summers at the National Music Camp in Interlochen, Michigan. Lori later returned as a counselor. During their college summers they enjoyed teaching their mother's students while she was on workshop tours.

Lisa and Lori are now independent piano teachers and active in their local music teacher organizations.

Lisa Bastien teaches in the preparatory department at Loyola University and in her home studio in New Orleans, Louisiana. Her Bachelor of Music in Piano Performance/ Pedagogy is from Drake University (Des Moines) and her Master of Music in the same area is from Arizona State University. While at ASU Lisa was instrumental in establishing the School of Music's preparatory department. Lisa is married to Basil Hanss.

Lori Bastien established a full class of students in Houston prior to returning to La Jolla, California to do the same. She attended the University of Redlands (California) for two years before transferring to Rice University (Houston) where she received a Bachelor of Music in Piano Performance. Lori is married to Eric Vickers.